Meditate Your Way to Success

Meditate Your Way to Success

The Definitive Guide to Mindfulness, Focus and Meditation

How Meditation is an Integral Part of Success and Why You Should Get Started Now

Your Path to Success: A Five Part Series

Chase Andrews

Copyright © 2017 by Chase Andrews

All rights reserved. No part of this publication may be reproduced, distributed, or transmitted in any form or by any means, including photocopying, recording, or other electronic or mechanical methods, without the prior written permission of the publisher, except in the case of brief quotations embodied in critical reviews and certain other noncommercial uses permitted by copyright law. For permission requests, write to the publisher, addressed "Attention: Permissions Coordinator," at the address below.

Chase Andrews

chaseandrews@thepassiveincomemachine.com

www.thepassiveincomemachine.com

Make sure to check out the rest of the books in this series:

Fail Your Way to Success: The Definitive Guide to Failing Forward and Learning How to Extract the Greatness Within - Why Failing is an Integral Part of Success and Why You Should Never Fear it

https://www.amazon.com/dp/B0738WDK6W

Discipline Your Way to Success: The Definitive Guide to Success Through Self-Discipline - Why Self-Discipline is Crucial to Your Success Story and How to Take Control Over Your Thoughts and Actions

https://www.amazon.com/dp/B0741FMCRX

Ask Your Way to Success: The Definitive Guide to Success Through Asking - How to Transform Your Life by Learning the Art of Asking

https://www.amazon.com/dp/B074CJPFMH

Believe Your Way to Success: The Definitive Guide to Believing and Your Path to Success How Believing Takes You from Where You are to Where You Want to Be

https://www.amazon.com/dp/B0747N14KF

This book is dedicated to those that want to smash through the glass ceilings they have put over themselves. Greatness is already within you, you just need to learn how to release it. This book will teach you exactly how to extract every ounce of greatness you have, and then some.

Preface

Introduction

Chapter One - Meditation in the Context of Success

   The Body

   The Mind

   A Higher Power

Chapter Two - An Introduction into the Universe

Chapter Three - Overview of Meditation

   Mindfulness

   Space and Time

   Mindfulness from Space and Time

Chapter Four - How to Invoke Mindfulness

   Exercises in Mindfulness

   Stage One

   Stage Two

   Stage Three

Chapter Five - Focus

Chapter Six - The Idea of Meditation

   Asking

   Being Open

Chapter Seven - Success

Chapter Eight - Greatness

   The Path to Greatness

Chapter Nine - Meditation

   Stage One

    Stage Two

    Stage Three

Chapter Ten - Meditation and Success

    Being Successful

Conclusion

Supplement: Meditation Guide

Preface

"Meditation ... is listening to the divine within"

Edgar Cayce

Most people confuse the true nature of meditation, and thereby inadvertently box the power of meditation into a space reserved for spiritual and religious phenomenon. They further set themselves up for a fall by buying into the notion that meditation is about being sedate - the exact opposite of what you need if you are ramping up for success.

Meditation is neither sedate nor spiritual. It is the medium that is whatever you need it to be. If you enter it with the desire to achieve some form of Zen, then that's what it will be. If you enter it with the desire for peace, that's what will await you. If you enter with questions, you will leave with answers. If you enter with the burning desire for success, you will find your greatness.

Success is one-third divine inspiration, one-third mental determination, and one third physical exertion. Any two out of the three, or less, will not do. Most people only know how to manifest the last - physical exertion. These are the folks that end up only being able to offer the world a contribution of hard physical labor. The prerequisites here are a strong and able body.

People who have the necessary mental determination and requisite physical determination mostly end up being strong middle-manager types who can bring about outcomes through hard work in others and in themselves. These are the drill sergeants of the world.

Finally, there are those who have the inspiration to see things others can't and to bring about changes in ways no one else can imagine. Not only can these people work hard, but they can use their mental fortitude to pick themselves up when they fail. But much more, they are also the people who can see beyond the horizon and together with a strong mind and a strong back, use their inspiration can change the world for the rest of us. These are the beings of greatness.

Finding the strength in your arms and in your back is fairly easy. It doesn't take a lot, except perspiration and repetition. It even gives us a certain kind of pleasure to build up and bulk up, then put that muscle to work. That's the entry level. If you want to take it up a notch, you go on to build your mind. You have to advance your knowledge - at least at the rudimentary level.

At that point comes the most important part of it all - to find the divine inspiration. This is where people make the mistake of thinking that you either have it or you don't. That is not true at all. Even if you do not have inspiration, you can find it. Just like, if you don't have muscle, you can build it. If you don't have the knowledge, you can acquire it. When it comes to inspiration, you need to find it within you and that's where meditation comes into play.

Introduction

"Meditation is not a means to the end, it is both the means and the end."

Jiddu Krishnamurti

The Romans had a saying back in the day when they ruled the civilized world. At a time when their influence spread across diverse cultures over significant distances, the Romans built their reputation on living large, bringing order and fighting for what they believed in. If they were here today, as a culture, they would be the titans of the business world, no doubt. For their ways and means are exactly what the hard-hitting, efficient CEO and inspired entrepreneur need to be these days to consistently make it to the top and stay there.

The one rule of thumb the most successful of the successful Romans lived by is this:

"Bis vincit qui se vincit in victoria"

It simply means that he who conquers himself in the hour of conquest conquers twice. There are many interpretations of this but the one meaning that encapsulates them all tells us that to be able to conquer anything, be it kingdoms or wealth, enemies or competitors, what one needs to do is to be in control of his own devices without giving in to his distractions.

In today's world which is filled with distractions, success is determined, not just by how much we work and how inspired we are. It is also about how strong our ability to resist distractions and deviations.

In many cases, the story of success forgets to mention the things that need to be avoided and focus is only placed on the things that need to be acquired or accomplished. Yes, indeed, meditation is a requirement that brings about a number of changes and fortifications in the human condition, but more than that, it also aligns the field of vision toward the objective and protects it from the distractions so many falls it is prone to.

Meditation provides a more powerful aid in the ability to stick to things and helps you navigate through hardships. Meditation is the fountain of a higher knowledge that is there when you need to make decisions based on incomplete data sets.

Einstein said that "*No problem can be solved from the same level of consciousness that created it.*" and that is the reason you need meditation, which is what he was talking about when he referred to a higher sense of consciousness. When you do not have the benefit of this higher consciousness, you are left to solve the problems you face with exhausting effort. It's a lot easier, a lot more efficient, and a lot more profitable to get solutions to your problems when you are shaped by the meditation that you practice.

Meditation paves the way to divine inspiration. In this context, divinity has to do with the cosmic energy, not the existence of an omnipotent being, commonly referred to as God.

Whether you believe in the existence of God, or you don't, it doesn't matter when it comes to meditation. If you have been working hard, trying to build your success from scratch, and you find that there is a glass ceiling that seems to be preventing further ascent, and you wonder how the Jobs and Bezos of the world do it. Well, you're about to find out.

***

Chapter One - Meditation in the Context of Success

"I meditate so that my mind cannot complicate my life."

Sri Chinmoy

Do you meditate? If you don't, then it's time to reevaluate your entire strategy to life and your pursuit of success. As it stands, if you are not meditating, it is very likely that you are missing many of the parts that will get you the superior outcome for the correspondingly appropriate level of effort. It is also highly likely that if you are not meditating, you are constantly hitting up against a brick wall of failure and having to run two lives - one that is focused on the objective, and the other where you are constantly cleaning up after failures.

There are two ways you can succeed in life. Success can be yours either by allowing the consequence from failure point you in the right direction, or you can get the answers you need to take the right path and achieve what you need without encountering the consequences of your failures.

Don't get me wrong. Failure is not bad - it is the greatest teacher there is. It is there to beat the secrets of the universe into you so that when you aim for something you, you end up getting it. But meditation takes a different tack. Meditation prepares you to receive the whispers of the universe around you so that when you make choices, they are the correct choice. You just know, almost instinctively, what to do in every particular situation.

The single most powerful practice a person can undertake is meditation. If you subscribe to the school of thought that meditation is about calmness, Zen, and peace, or about prayer, devotion, and spirituality, then there may be a reason for some of you to shy away. But meditating is neither religious, nor spiritual - it can be if you wish it, but by itself, it is what it is.

One way to view meditation is to equate it with a force that brings harmony to competing systems of the body and mind. The will of the body always seems to go in one direction, while the will of the mind always seems to go entirely in the opposite one. Many times we give in to one or the other and feel a sense of remorse that is nothing short of distracting. But the debate between the two can be chaotic and distracting. One of the effects of meditation is that it aligns your competing systems and brings harmony to the chaotic voices. That removes distraction and brings peace to the whole.

Have you ever had the chaos of a raging debate, between reaching for a cigarette or not, barely twelve hours after you quit? The battle that goes on is between your body that craves the nicotine, and your mind that made the decision to quit cold turkey; or, the debate of wanting to buy the latest sports car. One side of you wants to put you behind the wheel, while the other side is telling you that the right thing to do would be to save the money and instead get something you can afford.

Every single person has been in numerous pairings of opposing forces in their life. Sometimes we give in to one force, other times we prevail with the other. Whichever decision we make, the future that stems from that decision is colored with the consequences of that action. Not taking that cigarette puts you on the path to one set of consequences, breaking your promise to quit, puts you on another path. We've all experienced that.

If you look closely at these battles and chaotic arguments, you will begin to see that there is a third actor on that field of battle - a silent umpire of sorts. Some people call it a conscience, others call it the soul. But those words carry with it significant baggage that distracts from this discussion of meditation and success. For now, let's refer to it as our 'core'. However, you first need to identify what we label as the body, and what we label as the mind.

The Body

The body - which is actually still part of the primitive brain and the nervous system - is the one that is advocating your raw instincts. It is based on hunger and reward. It is a chemical equation. When your body wants you to do something, it creates a hunger in you that is palpable. The emotion in that is rather unpleasant and as we are instinctively wired to rectify whatever makes us feel unpleasant which drives us to go about finding the solution. For example, thirst and water; erection and sex, hunger and food. When you give in to what the body wants, it rewards you with pleasure - even to the point of flooding the rest of your brain with feel-good neurotransmitters like dopamine.

It's hard to walk away from this carrot and stick approach.

The Mind

On the other side of the equation is the mind. The mind is just sets of neurons that are functional in all the experiences and teachings you have gained throughout your life that has been schooled in what's good in the long term and what can be detrimental. Unlike the reactive and primitive part of the nervous system, we think of the mind as something more advanced and sophisticated. There are complex processes that can appreciate subtleties and different shades of right and wrong, good and bad, unlike the primitive minds, strictly binary algorithm.

To be clear, both sides of the equation are just different parts of the same brain. Even when we label it as the body, it is not really the body that does it; it is actually a part of the brain that is deeply entrenched into anything and everything we do.

You see, when animals and insects first evolved, there was no brain to speak of. There was just a simple central and peripheral nervous system that behaved on reacting to stimuli. Over millennia, that system adapted to become our primary instincts and is responsible for preparing our bodies to act in different ways. When you are in danger, have you ever realized that you can't seem to think? Most people can't think their way out of much when they are in fear or when they have a panic attack. That's because the part of your brain that is overpowering everything is the animal instinct in you.

As we evolved, we started developing higher thought and even imagination. We could foresee and we could plan. But all those developed in parts of the brain that grew on top of the part of the brain that drives us with instincts. The reason you can't seem to think or move when you are in fear or panic is that the lower brain functions control the rest of you. It can freeze you, animate you and do all of this independently from rational thought.

When your body craves sugar, or that sports car, or that smoke, it's about the body that is actually controlled by the primitive part of the brain. When you try to overrule it, it is coming from logic and conscious processes.

When those are at odds- and they are for most of our lives, the inner tussle can be a noisy affair - noisy enough to distract you from what you really need to get accomplished in the world that is outside the boundaries of your skin.

A Higher Power

It was mentioned earlier that there is one more actor on this stage that sees the constant battle between your mind and body. That actor is the one that realizes the two parts exist. It is the part of you that realizes there is a voice of reason and a voice of indulgence. The third actor on this stage, in many cases, is that part of you that is reading this text.

We face challenges in trying to distinguish which actor to follow with the next course of physical action - do we pick up that cigarette? Do we do finalize deal? Do we hire this person?

One way to identify the actors is to detect the method of their communication - their language so to speak. The language of your reasoned thought is the language you primarily converse in. If you are an English speaker, your reasoned thought communicates in English.

On the other hand, your primitive side - the body - speaks in feelings of discomfort and of bliss (the stick and the carrot). It doesn't communicate in any verbal language, and if you can hear the voice say things like "I don't feel comfortable' - that's just your rational mind interpreting your primitive brain and giving you the ability to communicate that outwardly.

The actor in the middle who watches both, the impulsive instinct and the logical thinker, has its own language to - it is the language of silence. The language is usually drowned out by the chaos and noise of the outside world and the incessant battle that rages between the voice and the feeling.

The one problem in all this is that the voice, when it releases a command or a suggestion, sounds a lot like the voice of the body. It's more of a feel - a gut feel, than meaningful words and structured sentences. It sounds nothing like the language of the logical mind. This causes a problem because whenever you act on the instructions of this silence and things work out right, you credit the feeling (the language of the primitive mind) for it and you start to doubt logic. When logic is right, you think it's the feeling that let you down. We all have this massive confusion playing in us and it gets worse over the years, especially for those who do not learn to sort it out or meditate.

The problem is that the three actors have different purposes, and wisdom is what teaches us to choose which to listen to. But when it comes to business, career, and other sophisticated areas of our life, the last thing you want is a primitive actor calling the shots or a logical actor who has less than all the facts to direct your action.

The actor that is the most reliable in executing higher functions, from business decisions to relationship decisions, is the actor who communicates through the medium of silence. I am hard pressed to call it a soul, but I am also aware of the baggage that term carries. It is really a form of energy that has no particular shape or form and does not reside in any particular organ. It's everywhere.

That soul is not a ghost-like spirit that we are used to seeing on TV. That soul is part of an uninterrupted energy that flows in us around us, and within everything in the universe. Have you heard about the law of attraction? Well, there are many permutations and versions of it. You should listen to talks by Alan Watts, or motivational videos by some of the other proponents of the Law of Attraction, and what you will start to realize is that all those times when the Law made no sense to you, was because you were missing the key piece of information that unlocks everything.

That key piece of information you need to know is that your soul is the energy that is part of a larger body of energy and when you speak the right language you vibrate that across the universe. It's that simple. Meditation gives you that vibration; in fact, it allows you that specific frequency of vibration, the frequency of silence.
■■■■■■■■■■■■■■■■■■■■■■■■■■■■■■■■■■■■■■

Chapter Two - An Introduction into the Universe

"You exist in time but you belong to eternity."

Anonymous

At its most fundamental level, this universe is made up of energy. From this energy, comes matter. From matter, come the various particles, and from particles we get elements. If you take hydrogen, you find that it is made up of one electron and one proton – two different particles. If you added another particle to that existing Hydrogen atom, you get Helium. And so you get one element after the other. But the starting point is the same – energy.

Einstein figured this out when he derived the *$e=mc2$* equation. You've seen it everywhere; you see it all the time. You probably even realize that it means that mass and energy are interchangeable. But it is also more than that. Matter and energy are the same things in different states. It's like saying that water vapor and ice are both the same, only that they are in different states.

From a superficial perspective, ice is tangible; you can hold it, observe it with your senses and even count it if it is cut into small cubes. Vapor on the other hand (in the absence of equipment) can't be seen, touched or measured with your bare senses. So for the purpose of this discussion let's admit that water vapor is intangible.

Energy and matter present the same parallel. Matter is tangible and energy is not (again, in the absence of special equipment). Your body is the same. It is composed of tissue and soul. Tissue is tangible and the soul isn't.

This world is built on tangible and intangible. The tangible are the parts you can observe while the intangible are the parts you cannot observe directly but you know they are here because of the way other elements or matter behave around them.

What has all this got to do with meditation?

Well just as sound is tangible, silence is intangible. So if we wanted a nice little package, here is what we have – matter, water, and the tissue of the body can be placed under the tangible column; while energy, vapor and soul are placed in the intangible column.

Sounds are tangible by virtue of the fact that you can use one of your senses to detect them. Feelings are tangible too because feelings are merely chemical reactions in your body that result in a certain level of detection. However, silence is undetectable by any sense in your body and only discernible by exclusion. For this reason, silence is considered intangible.

Energy, the soul, and silence are in the same column since they are intangible. We take the soul to be the part of the universal energy that is within us. So when you want to understand the soul and the universe by extension, you have to use silence. But that is a whole lot easier than it sounds. It's not sufficient to stop talking or stop listening. Invoking this brand of silence requires a different method, and that is the method of meditation.

The distractions of the mind that are constantly battling with the body are distractions that overshadow the silence of the soul. To reach that silence, you have to silence the chaos of the mind. This is the reason most people misunderstand meditation to mean the quieting of the mind. You actually have to still the mind before being able to appreciate meditation.

***

Chapter Three - Overview of Meditation

"Meditation is the tongue of the soul and the language of our spirit. "

Jeremy Taylor

Meditation is not as complex as it is made out to be and it is not as hard to achieve as you may have been led to believe. Your natural state is a state of silence and so meditation will come naturally to you if you take the time to get back to it.

We get much of our perception of the world from the senses we possess. We see, hear, smell, and so on. On their own, none of them really means anything. On their own, our senses are really just sending electrochemical signals to our brain and it is our brain that translates what it is and what it means. Whether it is sight, sound or smell, if we have no prior introduction, we would have no idea what we are looking at or what we are smelling. We sense non-binary data through association.

Binary data is the kind of data that can only be one or it's opposite. 1 or 0; Yes or no; on or off; and right or wrong. There are no shades of gray and in-betweens. In the beginning, the central nervous system was only capable of these binary processes. But we evolved, and a few million years later, we were able to conjure more complex thoughts and thinking patterns. That thinking pattern even allowed us to be able to predict future events based on present factors. Our brain becomes more able as it developed the mind and the mindsets that were built on top of that. We could even turn the observation on to ourselves and learn who we are and what we are about and we could finally turn consciousness back onto itself and ask the questions that elevated our existence. This higher level of thought is nothing short of amazing.

But at the back of all that, right down there at the base of the skull sits the ancient part of our brain that is still calling some of the shots when certain circumstances present themselves. One of those hardwired events that results in fear is facing the unknown. Fear is a powerful primary emotion that developed to keep prey alert for its predator. That still sits with us today and can disrupt our entire thought process and the outcomes that follow. However, if you can learn how to tap into your soul (again, there is no religious reference attached to the meaning of the soul) then you can overcome the crippling nature of fear.

As we set out to take a journey across the landscape of this book, you need to understand its final purpose. This book is about making you all that you possibly can be. This book is about returning the power into your hands. It is about energizing you by showing you the source of limitless potential and understanding - it is about reaching an awakening. It is about showing you that there is a teacher within you that you can tap onto. If you can look there and ask, whatever you ask for will come your way.

Meditation is not about lighting candles and closing your eyes in a serene and passive way. That is not meditation. Silence is not powerless; in fact, silence is one of the most powerful resources. If you can tap into that, all you ask for, the greatness you envision and the power that you need, are yours for the taking.

There are three steps that make the path to success. It is this path that you must learn and internalize if you are to truly escalate your abilities and elevate your life from here to greatness in one lifetime.

The first step is the development and execution of mindfulness. The second is the development of the discipline required to focus. The final step is the various levels of meditation.

Once you can undergo these steps effortlessly, there is nothing earthly that you cannot accomplish when you set out to do it.

Mindfulness

There is a lot of literature on the practice and discipline of mindfulness. And just like there is the unfortunate misunderstanding of what meditation is, there is even more misunderstanding of what mindfulness is.

You need to know three things to be able to make use of mindfulness as a step to meditation. The first is that mindfulness is about organizing space and time. The second is that mindfulness is about the alignment of your conscious mind with your current space and time. Finally, mindfulness is about expanding your conscious ability, which begins weak, and if built up can enlarge to great power.

There are two cosmic phenomena that this book will introduce you to so you can understand the scope of your mindfulness and how it ties in with the entire universe.

Space and Time

Space and time are two measures of an environment that spread across the universe. Beyond the boundary of the universe, the dimensions of space and time cease to exist. The energy that defines the expanse of this space and time is what gives rise to matter and all that comes from the existence of matter.

Space is beyond what your ruler can measure, and time is more than what your clock measures. We know that Einstein theorized, and physicists have proven since then, that time is an individual phenomenon and not standardized across space.

It would not make too much sense to delve too deeply into the physics and nuances of time except to say that we need to look at time as a stream. The analogy of the stream works in a number of ways, but it is not one that you should get carried away with. It holds its purpose here, but beyond this, it can be counter-productive.

The reason we look at time as a stream here is that time flows in one direction, and this knowledge is important in the quest to remain mindful. Second, that time can be as wide as a river or as narrow as a stream and the width of time that you can see, depends on how expansive your conscious mind can be. The final reason the river analogy works is that it allows you to see things that happen across space as a passage of time - just as the passage of the river.

Mindfulness from Space and Time

There are millions of phenomena and events that are going on around us. Imagine if you could have a screen looking at everything going on in the universe today - from the hatching of a fly to the birth of a star in a distant sector of the universe. That's a large number of data streams - a very wide river.

On the other hand, imagine if you just have one screen and that one screen only shows you your breathing. Nothing else, and as far as you can see, the entire universe, to you, is reduced to one act - the movement of air in and out of you. The first resembles an infinitely wide river with large amounts of data; the second represents a very narrow river. If our capability is limited to be able to comprehend and have a handle of just one stream, but you are given a mighty river to handle, your mind crashes. You become overwhelmed and you can't fathom your surroundings.

The problem with being overwhelmed is that the moment you do, the circuit breakers in your head break and you can't process your surrounding and whatever is facing you. We know that feeling all too well. The moment you can't understand your environment, a primitive emotion takes over and that is the emotion of fear. People are built to naturally fear things they do not understand. When you are overwhelmed, you will end up in a state of fear, or in some people that can even lead to anxiety and panic attacks.

By invoking mindfulness, you will be able to decrease the data stream and alleviate the feeling of being overwhelmed. Mindfulness is not just about focusing on one thing at a time, as most people will tell you online. Mindfulness is to focus on exactly what your breadth of stream allows. Most people start with just one thing at a time. You can do the same, then once you have practiced it for some time, you will find that you can indeed multitask - just doing it one thing at a time. The key is that your thoughts and your actions are one.

The crucial thing about all these is that the thing you focus on should be in the present. It should never be about the past and never about the future. And since you can only be in one place at one time, you will automatically focus on the place that you are in, at the time you are in. When you do that, the entire breadth of your stream is applied to the moment of time.

When bringing your entire mindfulness to bear on one thing and not forward or backward in time, what you are able to do is to look at the one thing in a way that is deeper than just the superficial characteristics of the matter. As you develop your mindfulness, you will find that you are able to penetrate the subject of your attention deeper and gain visceral understanding.

The more you practice that, the more you will strengthen, or in this case, widen that stream. When you widen that stream, more of you can be applied to the moment than you did before. This will continue to grow and you will continue to see things and observe things that you were once not able to.

The size of your stream compared to another person's stream is always going to be different. Some people can handle more in their conscious mind in one moment of time than another person can in that same moment. When you practice mindfulness, you start to expand that.

***

Chapter Four - How to Invoke Mindfulness

"The present moment is the only time over which we have dominion."

Thích Nhất Hạnh

It is rather simple to be able to get started with mindfulness. You can do this almost anywhere and while doing anything. After all, practicing mindfulness is just about doing and thinking about the same thing at the same time and going deeper into its processes, rather than going wider. But if you insist on being more disciplined about it, then grab a comfortable chair, and have a seat. Close your eyes (this is to cut off visual distractions) and direct your attention to the air that enters and exits your nose. Your breath is a natural metronome that allows you to bring chaos back into rhythm. This is a time-honored practice and you should feel very comfortable doing it.

Do not control the tempo of your breathing; instead just let your body do what it does best. You just have to sit back and watch it. If you have trouble watching it, then sit back and count it. One for in and the same for out. Keep counting to ten, and then start again. After you get the hang of it, you can stop the counting and just observe your breath.

Once you can do the short sessions, it's time to expand your abilities. The next step is to take the sessions from your couch to real life. You can apply mindfulness to everyday tasks, from the time you wake up to the time you go to bed. If you can transplant the same practice from breathing to doing other things, you will find that you are able to do them more efficiently and more accurately.

At this point, mindfulness will come naturally to you and you will find how much more you absorb at every waking moment of your life. You will also find that you do not even need to take notes in a meeting because you will be able to remember them just by being mindful of those who you listen to. You will also find that you have the ability to remember names and faces. Your capacity would have a marked increase.

Even once you are able to be mindful, you should still practice it on your own on a daily basis. Mindfulness is not meditation, even though it is used as a path to meditation. But it is a discipline of its own that you use to sharpen other areas of your psyche and mind.

Exercises in Mindfulness

There are three exercises that you can use to develop and maintain your ability to be mindful. In the event that you graduate mindful training and get to the point of successful meditation, there will still be days you will need the extra help to be able to meditate. A day will come where you will not be able to meditate or be focused. That's when you will find these exercises helpful.

Stage One

Breathing. We covered this earlier and it is usually enough to get you going. But here is another way you can use breathing to get more entrenched in mindfulness.

You can be anywhere for this. It doesn't matter if you or on a train, or in a coffee shop. You can keep your eyes open or closed for this, that's up to you. First begin inhaling deeply, then pause followed by a controlled release. Do this three times and, each time you do it, pay full attention to the point of your nose that meets the bridge just beneath your forehead. Imagine yourself looking at that spot. If your eyes are open, it would almost seem that you are cross-eyed.

As you look at that spot and complete three sets of deep inhalation, return to normal breathing with your eyes closed. Count each breath up to 10. Then start at zero again. Count again, up to 9. Then return to zero. Count again, up to 8. Then back to zero. If you lose track - start all over again, from 10. This should take you about five minutes, but each person is different and you shouldn't hasten or retard your breathing to keep within this time. Relax and do it at your own pace.

When you finish, and you open your eyes, you will be amazed to find that your disposition changes and eventually your position on things seem fresh. You will be tempted to take it all in, but try to apply your fresh state to the thing that requires your attention.

Most successful entrepreneurs who do this get straight to work on areas that need their creative powers. Or they do it before a workout.

Stage Two

The next level that you can try is a lot less involved but requires you to get an app for your smartphone, or you could just set a recurrent alarm for every minute. In this exercise, have a bell chime at specific intervals. Personally, my phone chimes gently, every twenty minutes. Twenty minutes is my magic interval and seems to work well for me. I am sure that will change as time passes.

Twenty minutes has been my thing because it is my natural window of efficiency. Whatever I get done usually only takes 20 minutes. And at that point, I am making sure that my focus is refreshed and renewed for one of two things. In some cases, it is usually time for me to get to the next task: Or it's time to inhale and tighten-up my mindfulness for the same task.

I have found this to be invaluable in getting my efficiency up. A number of us who practice this have found that there is no correlation between our effective window, but one thing that has held to be true is that each persons are different.

At the point the alarm chimes, close your eyes, take three deep cleansing breaths. Once it's done, get back to what you need to be doing.

Stage Three

This stage requires that you learn a new practice. This is the stage where you bring mindfulness to your entire life. Not just every evening, or every hour. This is to get you to convert your time to a full-on nature where you are not in one place while your feet stand elsewhere. You need to be in the same place your thoughts are. Planning the future is not considered going against this, neither is evaluating the future of something you are considering. These are all willful directions of the mind. The point is that you are not thinking about something other than what you are doing.

You do this by making sure that stage one and stage two are easily done. That takes time and practice. It takes diligence on your part to make sure that these things become habits. The ability to form a habit is useful but that habit is not about doing things on autopilot, the habit is about reminding you what you need to do at a particular time.

You start your day by reminding yourself that you will spend the entire day in a state of mindful focus (the focus part will come later). You tell yourself that this is your path to success and it requires the least amount of effort but has the most amount of bang. From that point, you stay mindful in everything and you be ruthless about it. Your path to meditation and mindfulness is not about making you tame like a rabbit. It's meant to make you as devastating as a lion.

Nothing about this meditation and mindfulness is meant for you to mistakenly think that you are about to become meek and nice. It's not. You need to wake up that lion in you that will set your sights on one thing and get it. This is how success stories are created.

Every time you catch yourself drifting, get yourself back to where you need to be. Use the breathing exercise to do it. If you find that you are distracted, do a short workout to burn up the energy and get your circulation going then focus on that heavy breathing. As you feel the intensity grow, focus your calm on to that. It's a form of energized calm that you will learn to appreciate once it starts working for you.

***

Chapter Five - Focus

"Concentrate all your thoughts upon the work at hand. The sun's rays do not burn until brought to a focus."

Alexander Graham Bell

The one thing we can never stress enough about when it comes to school or work is focus. Focus is the one thing that you must have to be able to get in the door to doing anything worth doing. If you can't focus on one thing, you are not going to be able to get through it without disengaging your brain from absorbing the information.

Focus is usually looked at as the ability to do one thing at a time from the starting point to the finishing line. That's a pretty fair description and you can see how you can build from your mindfulness techniques to get into a state of focus.

There are some differences between mindfulness and focus, and they are not entirely interchangeable.

Remember, focus is about doing one thing at a time without allowing yourself to get out of it till it's done. Mindfulness, on the other hand, is about applying your bandwidth to a task and looking at it deeper. When focus goes hand in hand with mindfulness, mindfulness is easier to invoke at the drop of a dime and you become more adept at switching on your mindfulness.

As common as it sounds, most people are not able to be mindful in what they do, and most people do not understand the real meaning of focus. Most people tend to rely on auto-pilots and apply their minds to something different than what their hands are doing or what their eyes are observing.

Focus is the ability to stick with it and narrow your resources to just one spot. While mindfulness deepens your field of knowledge, focus narrows it. Mindfulness without focus is not optimal, while focus without mindfulness yields nothing.

When you combine the two, you find out that all of a sudden, you have almost superior powers of observation. You don't even need to memorize things but you will remember it because of the focus you apply.

While it has been seen that mindfulness requires practice, focus on the other hand requires something completely different. Focus requires discipline and that takes time to build for those who have no idea of discipline.

If you are one of those who are not acquainted with discipline, you need to get to it now. Be assured, it is nothing like what you heard your parents and teachers talked about. The older generation uses the word and the concept behind it to illicit servitude and obedience. Whenever you don't obey them they blame it on some deficit in discipline. Discipline here has nothing to do with that. Discipline is more about you now. It's about what you know you need to do versus what you want to do.

It comes back to what the body wants and what the mind wants. When you do things that are fun, the body enjoys it and rewards you with feel good hormones. When you have to work, it doesn't reward you. That is what you have to change. Your body is not trying to trip you up: it's just trying to do what it's supposed to, which is to conserve energy. It is there as a constant reminder that energy is scarce and that you need to conserve it. Having fun, on the other hand, requires fewer resources so you get rewarded for that.

But now, it is up to you to look past all that. You know for a fact that you have enough resources to do what you want and when you are in the mode to succeed, I don't know about you, but for me, it's always an attitude of do or die. I would rather work to the last breath in pursuit of my greatness than to relax. My underlying mindset has always been 'do or die'.

Discipline is a mental guardrail. You invoke it to say that you will do something at a certain point and that you will not waver from doing it. In this case, you say that you will focus on a task until a certain time in the future, or until a certain outcome is reached. That discipline is a contract you make with yourself and if you break that discipline for whatever reason, you are not being true to yourself.

No matter what you say or do to others, make sure that you never kid yourself. You never lie to yourself and you never let yourself down. You must always live up to your own objectives, both in the long and short term.

Meditation and mindfulness work for everyone but it is not some magic wand that you wave while sitting on the couch. Your mental fortitude needs to be built up and needs to be enhanced over time.

In most cases, some people know what they need to do to get something, but they just don't have the discipline to constantly and consistently apply the work that needs to go into it because they are unable to overcome their own hurdles.

Of course, there are superficial ways to overcome it. You can listen to motivational videos and you can read inspirational quotes, but those are temporary cures and you should not rely on them all the time. The best thing you need to do is to be able to invoke discipline when you need and you should be able to apply it all times.

Discipline is the virtue that is going to see you through. Mind you, discipline is not about being uptight. It's not about being particular. It's about doing what you told yourself you would do. If you lack discipline, begin with a decision. Start small, and start fast. Tell yourself you are going to do something and then do it no matter what, without excuses.

The reason discipline is not something everyone has is that our weakness comes from lack of accountability and motivation. When we are left to do things on our own, we find that we can tell ourselves its ok and let our inaction off the hook. But you cannot do that, just as you are ruthless about your time, you have to be ruthless about your discipline as well. When you say you are going to do something, you hunker down till it's done. You do it for the big items and you do it for the small items and you do it for anything in between. The only time you let go of something that you decided to do is if you find a way that is better than what you planned.

Let's get back to focus. Focus can only happen if you decide to be disciplined about it. You need to be able to bring the discipline to bear on your focus. Any time you feel like doing something other than what you need to be doing, you must be able to halt that action and keep your mindfulness on the task at hand.

This is an important aspect of the entire process. If you leave discipline out of it, what you end up doing is being mindful about things that may not be of worth to your objectives. At the base of all this meditation and mindfulness exercises, remember that the idea is to use it to become a success and go beyond that to achieve greatness. You're not here to take on a vow of piety. You're here to put it everything on the line and change your world as you know it.

When you focus, as you have read thus far, you will realize that discipline is the key in your ability to keep your focus on the right path. If you allow your focus to wander, then your mindfulness that is charging ahead to look at things deeply will be looking at work one minute and looking at something else the next. That is never what you want. You want to look at one thing till you reach a milestone that you decide, would be the point you stop. The more you do this, the more you will be able to fine-tune your ability to understand yourself and understand your ability to focus and be mindful.

Let's assume that you now have an idea of how to be mindful and you have an idea of how to direct your focus. These are two skill sets that you can expand through the course of your life and you will see that there is no end to how much you can accomplish just by getting these two on par with your potential. But the thing about focus and mindfulness is that it resides in the tangible world. Remember earlier on we talked about the tangible and intangible sides of the equation. We looked at energy being intangible and matter being tangible.

We also looked at sound being tangible and silence being intangible and we left off by saying that meditation is the language of silence. Let's get back to that point and go deeper to see how that gets you to success and how that develops your place in time and space.

Focus and mindfulness are tangible because they are the result of chemical interactions in your brain. You are actually willing the chemistry of your brain to direct its focus without getting carried away to something else and you are directing your thoughts by the use of your breath to go deeper into something. Meditation is not any of these but uses them to achieve the state you need to be in.

Once you know how to focus on something and be mindful about it, you can even do it to silence. You can focus on silence, and you can go deeper into that silence to be able to achieve the state of meditation you need.

Silence, not just the absence of sound, is your quest at this point. And as with all relationships, your relationship with silence will take time to develop. This section of the book is designed to show you how to get acquainted with silence and advance your relationship with it.

***

Chapter Six - The Idea of Meditation

"The best way to meditate is through meditation itself. "

Ramana Maharshi

Your initial acquaintance with meditation will give you an introduction to silence and its nature. You will, in time understand the secrets of silence and the nature of it so that you can direct your efforts in ways that are the most effective and the most productive.

The Law of Attraction that you have undoubtedly heard of predicates its entire premise on the fact that you are able to attract anything you want from the universe. But the universe doesn't speak English, Latin or Sanskrit - or any other earth-bound language you can think of. It speaks in vibrations - specifically the vibration of desire that you can only effectively project on a backdrop of the silence that meditation can provide.

It's not just the law of attraction that relies on the silent backdrop of meditation; it's also the other way around. Only half your success is based on wishing or asking for things, the other half is based on understanding the opportunity that is placed in front of you. For this you need answers, you need blueprints for action and you do this by asking for advice on the nature of the challenge and the possible course of your action. You must not only be able to ask for an opportunity and attract it, you can also ask for direction and receive it. Meditation is a duplex channel. It is not always about receiving but also for presenting.

Meditation can make you as powerful as a lion or as meek as a rabbit. Meditation is about tapping the energy of the universe to get what you want. Remember that the basis of 'want' is conjured in the conscious mind and that is, many times, influenced by what you face in your physical environment. If you chose to desire based on that, you can, and you will get what you ask when you meditate. But here is a better way. Especially for those of you who do not know what to ask for, you can ask for the knowledge of what to ask for.

So the point of commencement in your asking exercise is to either ask for what you want - through vibration in a state of meditation or to ask for guidance on that which you are best suited to do. I have found that the later always results in a better end.

Asking

Asking is an art. You know the cliché, *"be careful of what you ask for"*. Well, there is tremendous truth to that, because the universe will always give you whatever you ask for and if you ask for something without understanding the full ramifications for it, you could be in a lot of trouble.

When I was very young, the story of King Midas was read to me and at first it was an awesome fantasy that one person could wish for something and get it and moreover, he could touch anything and turn it to gold. The part about touching his daughter and turning her to gold was lost on me for some time until one day I realized that that was an awful thing to happen. As my adult years came and time rolled on, that story stayed with me and I realized that among the different lessons of the story, the one that is most poignant is that you should be careful what you wish for. Then that realization matured and now I stand at the point of realizing that making a wish is not a simple matter.

We are very powerful in our current state. If you knew how to harvest it consistently, you will see that you could wish for anything and take the fruit of that wish and turn it into anything. But sometimes, we pay the consequences for the wishes we make and that throw us back a little and we regress in our advance forward.

Like Midas, we sometimes have to deal with catastrophe resulting from our wish. But there is a way out of that.

Like it was mentioned earlier, there are two ways of asking. The first is you ask for things that your conscious mind conjures. The problem with this is that the conscious mind is caught up asking for things that are fairly menial and influenced by the outside world. If you want to be more than what your world is, then you can't rely on your conscious mind to come up with the list of things to ask for. If you are relying on your conscious mind to come up with the list, you would have to spend a lot of time reflecting on what you want and that takes time and it eventually leads to a state where you find that almost all of what you mind asks for has no long term benefit that leads to greatness.

The second way of doing it is to meditate on asking for what to ask for. Yes, I know, it's kind of circular in its logic but if you put some thought into it, you will start to see the light.

When you ask the universe for guidance on what to ask for, the universe looks at what you are best suited for and tells you exactly what you need to get there. When you ask for those things and make use of them in this world, you suddenly find yourself achieving more than what you ever could than by just following your conscious mind to ask for something trivial.

You need to review in your head that you are a body that is capable of anything, even the things that you are not even ready to imagine or contemplate. If you look at some of the greatest minds in the world, you will find that the reason we hold them in such high esteem is that they did something that no one before them ever did.

For you to do something that no one else ever did, how could you possibly let your conscious mind, which is really looking to mimic and follow, come up with something unique?

When you are in business and you start off as an entrepreneur, venture capitalists who are looking to fund you are always going to ask you what you have that is different than what others are offering. If you told them that you are going to build another iPhone or another Corvette, it just won't cut it because you have no competitive advantage. You have no patents, and you have no inventions. To satisfy any of those needs, you should have something unique. The problem is the conscious mind struggles to find anything unique.

You have to rely on divine inspiration. That is what you get when you ask the universe for what to ask for. You find out that there are new frontiers where no mind has come to before. While meditation gets you halfway there, you have to apply massive action (which we will talk about in my book on Massive action to Success).

Being Open

Once you resign yourself to asking for what to ask, there will come a time that you will not like the answer. It may seem unpopular or not have the glamor you were expecting. But you have to be open about it and take it as it comes because greatness is a journey, not a stop. The arc of greatness takes you from nothing to everything and along the way, you pass stations that teach your self-control, discipline, meditation, desire, how to fail, and so much more before finally delivering the success that is fully baked and well deserved.

The part of you that may be unsatisfied is the part of you that is controlled by the conscious mind and the conscious mind can be easily swayed by things that you see and feel around you. It is even open to misunderstanding and misinterpretation. It is subject to envy and ego and it is subject to persuasion by the primal instincts that it battles constantly.

The universe that you connect with in the midst of meditation has no such limitation and no such error that arises to cause a stumble. If it is an idea born of divine inspiration you can be absolutely certain that you will be safe in the idea that strikes and it will lead you to the success that you can imagine.

***

Chapter Seven - Success

"Many of life's failures are people who did not realize how close they were to success when they gave up."

Thomas A. Edison

You want to be a success. I get it. We all do. But are you willing to do all that is necessary to get you there? Are you willing to do whatever it takes, walk however far, and climb however high you need to, to be able to get to the point you can consider yourself successful? And most important of all, once you get to the top are you willing to do it again? And again? And again? Can you find it in yourself to constantly extend the breadth and scope of your success?

How you answer those questions will depend on how much confidence you have in your dreams and the extent to which you value your ability. To most people, they want success because they confuse the rewards they see, with successes that they have no idea of achieving. Their limited vision of success is measured by the car or the jewelry they buy. This is a trap that you must stay away from. Do not ever confuse rewards with success. If you do, it is the path to getting yourself in a lot of trouble. If you confuse success with rewards, then there is a possibility that you will take the darker path to the rewards that entice you. This is what illicit gains are sparked by.

Numerous people I talk to who hear me rally against viewing things from the perspective of rewards tell me that if it is not about the rewards then what is the point of working and striving? I understand that point, and to answer it, you have to look at history to see what happens to the people who coveted the rewards to which they have no claim. Look at Emperor Nero of Rome. He did not deserve one ounce of the wealth he coveted and received and when he became mad with his own wealth the tragedy that befell him was severe.

On the other hand, look at Augustus Caesar, who was one of the richest men in the entire world at the time but lived in a simple part of the palace with simple fittings and ate enough to keep him healthy. He ruled wisely and was one of the longest serving emperors - remembered well to this day.

Rewards that come organically in the wake of successes are abundant and good. Rewards that come from coveting rewards, will lead to disaster. Understand your own motivations, towards rewards.

Success is the accomplishment of something that you set out to do. You set a goal that was beyond your ability, you understood all that led to it and you learned all you needed to and along the way you thought hard and worked hard at doing it. You made the dream a reality - that is not meant to be a small feat. That is the success you are aiming for. Success is the combination of tangible and intangible as well. Just like we saw in the beginning, tangible efforts are the one that you put your back into it and you perspire to pull it off. Intangible efforts are the inspiration that you have to mentally bring the physical action about.

Many people who fail, rely on one or the other, but not both, and they don't achieve their goal. When you ask for success, and you ask for the area that you should work on, divine inspiration will give you the answer you seek and the path to achieve it. But you still have to walk the path. The asking is the intangible and the walking is the tangible and you need to do both to be able to pluck success from the tree of greatness.

The part of success that is intangible gets a little tricky. If you don't get used to making success based on this part that is intangible, you are going to have to come up with significantly more stamina than you need to.

When you ask the universe, in a state of meditation, about what you should strive for, you will get the divine inspiration to do what needs to be done. But there is another way you can achieve success, and that is to look about you and think about what you would like to do (this comes from the realm of the conscious mind) and then ask the universe to lay that out or you. It will. But at this point, you are left pretty much to your own devices to get things done. You can still snatch success from the jaws of failure, but it comes at a price that's higher.

The price you pay comes in the form of more effort and more disappointment but you can still achieve it - without divine inspiration, the only way for you to gain success is through a brute force attack. That means you keep pounding it until you learn everything there is to learn about your objective and finally understand it in its entirety.

That takes time and many people don't have the mental fortitude and the psychological stamina to pull that kind of victory off. We can keep advocating failure as a path to success, and it is a valid path, but there is an easier and more efficient way if we take advantage of meditation.

Just to recap. There are three kinds of success that you can work on;

The first is the one that you get from desiring what your conscious mind comes up with, then, you just start hitting the pavement until you get it. You learn from failure and you put your back into it, relentlessly pursuing your dreams. You will succeed and you will attain greatness as long as you don't give up and you learn from each and every failure.

The second is when you meditate and you learn how to ask the universe and to attract the things you desire. When you do it this way, you are going to get what you desire but the nature of the successes, while invigorating and satisfying, will be comparatively shallow. These kinds of objectives are usually reward-oriented and that comes with its own consequences down the line. But do not misunderstand me, the success is nonetheless real.

Finally, you have the third kind of success where you derive your path based on attracting what best suits you, then build on that. You ask the universe for guidance on the best course of action and then you make your physical body do whatever it takes. In the midst of accomplishing, you continue to seek your guidance from the universe during your meditation sessions and you will find that every time you come to a point requiring a decision, your decision-making process is clearer and almost always right.

There are tradeoffs between one path to success and another. In the first, you straddle your physical and your divine self. In the second you exemplify the hard knocks that make you who you will become. In the third, you claim your divinity by surrendering to the universe and achieving greatness for it.

***

Chapter Eight - Greatness

"You were designed for accomplishment, engineered for success, and endowed with the seeds of greatness. "

Zig Ziglar

You don't start life by thinking you are going to be great. You have no concept of great when you are born and no concept of failure either. You are a blank sheet and you are shaped by your surroundings.

The reason you don't have any inclination of greatness is that you don't need to be told or you don't need to feel it in you to achieve anything that is great. You are great where you stand, now all that remains is that you get up and translate that into something tangible. As you stand, at the point of your life where questions about your own mark on this world arise, you start to think in terms of success and greatness and failure and loss. These are all terms that bring vivid thoughts and association to what you could become in the future. Either this or that. These thoughts start to get you on your way to self-discovery and you start to think about the factor of purpose.

A person's purpose is a funny thing. You, on your own, are neither the first person nor the only person that can be tasked toward a certain purpose. Many people get inspirations to do or build something. The get ideas to build something or invent a game changer. But they don't go about doing it because of one excuse or another. Then one day they see their idea in the shop window. Someone had done it and it's the next hot thing on the market.

Do you realize what happened?

What happened was that you had divine inspiration- there are times you will stumble upon this. But you did not put in the necessary effort or time to convert the intangible idea into a tangible product. You missed out, but the universe gave it to someone else, and that someone else picked it up and ran with it.

You are not the only person in the world that can communicate with the universe. You are not the only person in the world that will come up with the next game changer. But the one that does do the work is the one that snatches success from the dreamer who patted himself on the back for getting the idea but didn't lift a finger.

These are opportunities and opportunities themselves are intangible. You have to make things happen - you have to provide the effort, solve the challenges and bring the elements together so that you get to the finish line.

Remember you have two ways to do it. You can either hit yourself against the brick wall of failure and learn from it and eventually get to the right formula - which takes time, or you can get your answers through meditation and get there sooner.

The choice is up to you. Meditation is not a short cut - it's just more efficient.

The Path to Greatness

If success is so involved, then you must be thinking that greatness is a lot more. Greatness comes at the end of a string of successes. And I am not talking about how well your company's stock is performing or how many years it has beaten street expectations.

The path to greatness is not something you plan. It is something that results organically after you have consistently worked at success over the course of a lifetime. Greatness is typically awarded posthumously. Those who indeed do achieve greatness have learned so much from their efforts and toils on the way to success, that they are humble enough not to think themselves great. But in their heart, that greatness manifests as the feeling of deep contentment and humility that knows no parallel.

You cannot hope to achieve greatness overnight. It takes a lifetime. One of my most admired pillars in history is Alexander the Great, and I have read numerous books about him and his battles and the way he thinks. He went against the odds, taking a small band of fifty thousand men against the night army of one million, and eventually won.

There are many strategies that are accredited to him even till today. Many of those strategies are still taught at West Point. His father Philip II was no doubt a huge factor in teaching him but that was not enough to make the world bow in awe to this young king.

There was a passage in one of the books I read on the accounts of Alexander on the day of the largest battle he would face before conquering the Persian army. He was in his tent sleeping and was late for the battle. His General came calling and woke him up. He was curious how Alexander could have slept on the day of the largest battle of his life, with so much at stake. What stood in the balance were not just the lives of fifty thousand men, but also the future of Greece. Had he lost that battle there would be nothing from stopping anyone from conquering Greece and killing all the people he loved back home. The stakes were high that morning - but Alexander was calm. In response to his general's amazement at how he could sleep with such a day ahead of him, he simply said that the battle was already won and all they had to do was to show up for the fight. The battle was already won in the intangible realm, and now just remained to be fought in the physical.

Indeed, that day in Gaugamela, Alexander took his fifty thousand men and decimated the Persian army of one million. He then set chase to capture the fleeing Persian King Darius III.

The victory on that battlefield and many others before it, for Alexander, made him one of the greatest military tacticians. The night before that battle, he sat meditating in his tent. The contents of his appeal to the universe is anyone's guess, but for him to fall asleep after that, then wake up late the next morning and declare the battle already won tells me, and those who know the power of meditation intimately, that he knew exactly what he needed to do and what remained was just going out, getting skin in the game and doing it.

The path to Alexander's greatness was filled with successes on the battlefield. No person can ever doubt that hand to hand combat is the most visible of contests that pits one life against the other. Battles exemplify the contest and show how the participants give everything they've got. You have to visualize that in yourself. Of course, minus the gory, you must visualize the gut-spilling nature of hand to hand combat. But the rest of it is true. Each time you go up, you should commit everything. If you can do that and you are meditating on the eve of that battle and every day before it. There is nothing you can't win.

Each battle you win is a success. Each war you win is a greater success. And after a lifetime of winning, you are crowned great.

***

Chapter Nine - Meditation

> *"I can be stressed, or tired, and I can go into a meditation and it all just flows off of me. I'll come out of it refreshed and centered and that's how I'll feel and it'll carry through the day."*
>
> Ray Dalio

Let's get back to meditation. You need to know how to do it, and if you have already got an idea of how to focus and how to be mindful, then you will have an easier time in getting to meditation. I would advise against trying to meditate immediately and skip all the focus exercises and mindfulness exercises.

Meditation is a personal journey. What one finds and what one experiences are very different from one another. The effect and benefit of meditation also change with time. The longer one has been actively meditating, the greater changes over time they can expect to experience.

The greatest change in a person's life comes at the beginning when a sudden burst of clarity and the changes to the person's life materializes. The first year after meditation begins in earnest, will see the most change from the year prior.

There are three stages in the life of a person who takes up meditation seriously, and who continues in daily mindful reverence and focused attention. In a short amount of time, you will find that you can't get through your day without the time to meditate. It becomes your personal moment with something greater than just yourself. You will find that the answers to all you seek can be found in the time you meditate and the unnecessary pain you may incur from matters of the day can be surrendered during those times as well.

The three stages you encounter will span across your entire lifetime. The first stage is the point just a few short months after you begin and spans for a few years after that. There is no specific time frame. I have heard it takes as long as five years for some. I have also heard from those who have been in the first stage for just a year. It really does not matter how long you stay in stage one, or any stage for that matter. This isn't a classification system or a classroom. You need not worry about which stage you are. The mere purpose of describing it is to give you a heads up on what it will feel like.

Stage One

The first stage is marked by rapid increases in mental and emotional acuity. Even outside meditation times, you will tend to get a better grasp of things and go on to understand the nature of things that come across your path. You will find that you are on top of things and that nothing really surprises you, and you seem to have clarity of mind to an extent almost as though you foresaw every event that happens to you. You will also find that in this stage, you make the greatest progress and that you now have more energy in your life - not just mental energy, but also physical energy.

If you happen to combine meditation with fasting (and you don't have to) you will also find that your health and vigor increase and your mind and body have a youthful presence about them. The point is not to look young, but it's rather to extend your physical and mental capabilities.

Stage Two

In stage two, your acceleration in change will diminish. You will still experience changes, but in a seemingly more organic way, at a slower pace. You will find here that you have found a deeper meaning to your meditation and along with that, you have found deeper meaning to the things you have set out to accomplish. Mind you, all this meditation is in conjunction with people who are striving for success and not for the folks who are looking for serene spirituality. In stage two, you will find that much of what you experience at this point has also fortified your conscious mind and that meditation has managed to influence how you physical mind thinks.

In stage two you will start to advance your success to a degree that will seem superhuman to those who are not along for the ride. Don't be shy about it and don't be extravagant with it as well. Don't be surprised if you can will things into existence just by wanting it. Many people I meditate with show signs of clairvoyance in daily activity. They can join the pieces faster. They become formidable negotiators with this power and those who are not in the know when it comes to meditation, just can't seem to keep up when they come across a person who meditates, especially if that person is in stage 2.

Stage Three

After a brief change of pace in stage two, you will find that stage three will be a change in pace again, this time to one where you will see sudden and accelerated changes. The biggest change you will notice here is that you will be able to observe people and their intentions very clearly. If you think that you were able to conduct robust negotiations in the last stage, you will find that stage three is significantly better. You will find that distractions no longer exist and that you will be able to enjoy your life better than you ever have. You will understand things and you will be able to release all sense of fear because the realm of the unknown will gradually shrink. As you know, one of the greatest sources of fear is the unknown.

Aside from giving you an idea of what a life centered on meditation would be like, the three stages above should give you an idea of what you will gain from meditation. This is above and beyond the clarity that you need for the business decisions you make and the impact that you will have on your world.

***

Chapter Ten - Meditation and Success

"People think meditation is a huge undertaking. Don't think of it like that."

Deepak Chopra

The more you meditate, the less you will need failure to be your guide in areas of the unknown. For those who do not meditate, they learn by failing. While there is nothing wrong with failing, the one problem with it, aside from the heartache it sometimes causes, is that it delays you from reaching your intended objective.

In a book on failure, we talked about something called the FSG (Failure – Success – Greatness) matrix. The FSG matrix is the arc that takes you from desire and across failure, followed by success then followed by greatness after a lifetime of success. For those who do not meditate, this is a great way to do it. But the one thing that it consumes a lot of is time. In today's market, time-to-market is a critical component in the success of a venture. If you can't take your idea to market in a short period of time, you can bet that someone else will.

Meditation has indeed become the competitive advantage of CEOs and entrepreneurs. Without it, they spend too much time learning from mistakes that they wouldn't have had, had they just mastered the art of mindfulness, focus, and meditation.

There are three factors that determine if an entrepreneurial venture will be successful. The first is if the idea is patently new and proprietary, the second is if the idea solves a problem. Third, is if the idea can be converted to a working product that can be manufactured at a price point which the market will accept. If you think about it, this is a Herculean feat considering that there are a lot of variables that are unknown at the early stages of the game. Many people have ideas and those ideas seem plausible, but most of the time, making them marketable and appealing are insurmountable obstacles.

If you start to handle these problems with trial and error, someone is going to see it and take your idea and run with it. The only credible advantage that you have is the divine inspiration which inventors, that have made it big in the past, seem to have exhibited.

As much as there is hard work in doing what you have to do, there is also the razor sharp intuition that you must have in order to be able to define the market to address and have the intuition of how to engage it. All these come fairly easily when you are just a stage two meditation practitioner.

To be a powerful CEO or an effective entrepreneur, there are certain skills that you need and they are not taught in any MBA program. You need to be able to have such clarity of mind that you can see what's what without any room for error.

If you stand where you stand now and look at some of the top business leaders in the Fortune 500 or if you look at the top entrepreneurs in Silicon Valley, you may find what they do to be almost superhuman. Imagine what the man on the street thinks about someone like Jack Welch. Or Warren Buffet? Or even Jeff Bezos.

The level of activity that needs to happen to be able to organize such seemingly complex activity is something that you cannot do effectively and profitably if you do not have the power of meditation behind you. On the other hand, greatness is something that you can contemplate when your ability to meditate is as diligent and disciplined as your ability to get up and hustle.

Meditation is the most efficient discipline you could possibly engage in to be able to change the way you see everything and the way you engage the world of business and the realm of your personal life. Success defines us more in itself than the rewards that follow in its wake. When we enhance ourselves and our abilities with the benefit of meditation, the success that ensues, alters who we are at a fundamental level and, in time, catapults us into a higher plane of performance.

The enhancements, over time, are not geometric in their progression but rather most definitely exponential. These exponential gains reverberate across our faculties in areas that govern our emotional as well as intellectual abilities. It pervades our existence as a business leader, as an entrepreneur and an achiever as much as it alters the capacity of being a husband, a wife, a father, a mother and a community driver. Meditation is the Rosetta stone to the secrets of life and the secret that has been hiding in plain sight until now.

In the last few years, we have seen a trend among some of the top names occupying the C-suites across America and even in Europe. The trend has been to come out of the closet on a critical area of their success and their ability to create and deliver almost superhuman results. From here, it has become evident to all what few of us already know - that meditation is a powerful ally.

Meditation is the door that allows you to step into the real truth and knowledge of life and the universe. It is the missing link in the Law of Attraction, and it is the guide to those who have lost their ability to move from mere reactionary beings to become almost divine in presence and formidable in ability.

Oprah Winfrey, Jeff Weiner, Jerry Seinfeld, are all familiar names who pound the pavement hard every day while holding on to the power of meditation beneath the surface. They credit meditation as the source of their ability and success to meditation.

For those of us who meditate and go out into the world to make a difference, be it from the technological space, the education industry, the manufacturing sector - it really doesn't matter where, even in politics, meditation is the nexus between where we stand and the realm of the cosmic.

Being Successful

By no means should you ever think that being successful stops at meditation. That will never happen and if you try it, you are bound to lose and eventually tire out of expectation of meditation. Success that is consistent, hard-hitting and significant comes from doing real work. One of the most successful hedge funds, Bridgewater, run by Ray Dalia who is also an avid practitioner, attributes his success to meditation. He seems to have the right grasp of it when he says that it helps him, not just with anxiety and stress, but it is the source of his creativity. It helps him to see old things in new light and be independent in his thinking. But in addition to all this, Ray has a strong work ethic and is not shy to put his nose to the stone.

If you had to simplify the whole thing, you need two things in order to reach and claim superhuman success; the first is that you need the intangible force of meditation, and second is that you need the tangible force of hustle.

Meditation inspires you to action and gives you the direction to move in. You minimize failures and thereby increase your rate of success instead of spending time and energy fixing mistakes and learning from them. Meditation can even give you the ideas that will change the world, all you have to do is to put your back into it.

The human condition is the conduit between the cosmic and the earthly. What we imagine through divine inspiration transforms from intangible ideas to tangible reality by the force of our will and tirelessness of our labor. It is not enough to have ideas. It is not enough to have the desire, and it is insufficient to be laborious. All three must come together and gel.

Meditation is not only the nexus to the energy of the universe, but it is also the energy field that can bring all three together so that we are able to balance the forces and achieve true greatness.

***

Conclusion

"The purpose of meditation is personal transformation."

Henepola Gunaratana

As human beings, we are endowed with the greatest gift of all - the knowledge that we have the power of the divine within us. Our divinity, however, isn't a blind gift, it is given to those who recognize and desire it. The economics of the cosmos is such that what we desire doesn't come free but comes to us in the form of opportunity, gifts, and lessons. It is up to the will within us to put them all together and claim our achievement.

As simple as it is, we tend to be blinded by all that is thrown up in front of us. From entertainment to distractions, to low hanging fruit that simulates success but is actually fake in nature because in no way does it require our involvement to harvest.

Man's greatest success comes from the level of contribution he makes to mankind. The greatest of historical figures are the ones who made the most contribution to society and the world at large. In return they were rewarded - sometimes in fame, sometimes in gold, and sometimes, both. There have been many who have even been awarded posthumously without ever knowing the accolades that were awarded. In your quest for success and subsequent greatness, you will find that you are fulfilling a destiny that is of your choosing. Anyone can take up the challenge to be great, but we all need help.

The kind of help we need is not the kind which a friend can offer; it is one where you need to rely on nothing less than the power and presence of the universe itself. To be able to call upon that power is when you rely on meditation. Meditation is the language of the energy that is omnipresent in the universe. It is the energy that exists on every plane and every dimension. It is the source of space, time and every phenomenon we know, don't know and can't possibly imagine. When you ask, you will indeed receive. But make no mistake; what you receive is not a gift-wrapped box containing your wishes. When you ask, what you get is the will, the power, and the opportunity as well as all the answers to your questions. You just need to get up and make it happen.

If you don't know the skill set you need - meditate for the answer. If you don't know what to ask for, meditate for the guidance. If you don't know how to develop a product, mediate for the process The answer is to meditate, regardless of the question. Once you know how to turn to meditation, success is a hustle away.

***

Supplement: Meditation Guide

Set aside two 20-minute periods in your day when you are fairly certain that there will be no outside distraction. Typically, do this once in the morning before the sun rises and once in the evening.

The morning session should be done after your workout routine when your body is energized, and your mind is alert.

The evening session should be done before your supper and at least three hours before you turn in for the night.

I.   Begin with a warm-up period where you sit comfortably and let your mind race to whatever it wants. Let the mind do its thing, while you keep watch over it. Look at the thoughts the mind conjures, and do not judge those thoughts. If you remember to make a call or watch a program, don't jump up and proceed to undertake that task. Instead, let it go. Your only task is to watch your mind by watching the thoughts it generates. This warm up period should last between 3 and 5 minutes.

II.   Begin your mindfulness exercise of breathing. Start with three deep breaths. Inhale slowly paying attention to nothing but the breath that is entering you. Feel your lung expand, sit up straight if you feel you can take in more. Pause. Then, release your breath in a controlled and deliberate manner. None of this should be rushed or performed in a practiced, perfunctory manner. Exhale until there is no air that can exit on its own and do not attempt to force any extra air out. Let it be. Repeat these steps two more times.

III.   Once you have completed the deep breathing step, return your breath and its tempo to your body's natural rhythm. Do not attempt to control it, do not attempt to reduce or increase its pace. Keep your eyes closed and point your face directly ahead. Imagine watching the bridge of your nose and the air that is flowing in and out of it like waves washing on the shore. Gently as your breath enters like the incoming tide lapping the sand, and then gently ebbing as it retreats.

IV.   Watch this breath and count them each time it enters. Count to ten, making sure that your count does not hasten or retard your pace of breathing.

V.   The breathing exercises should last for 2 to 3 minutes, or perhaps more if you feel comfortable and alert.

VI. Reduce the counting as you progress from one set to the next. Your first set you counted to 10. For your second set, count to 9. Then, to 8. And so on until you come to 1. At this point treat every breath that enters and exits as one. Your breath is now a seamless exchange between you and the environment.

VII. Stay in this state. There is no need to count. There is no attention to your breath. The only thing you are focusing on is the silence that you know is deep within you. Look for that silence.

VIII. Remain in this state constantly fending off distractions by not turning to them to change them, but by intentionally paying attention to that silence within you.

IX. As you stay in this state where there is no thought, no concern, no anxiety, and no worry you will also notice that you are no different from the air you breathe, or space you occupy. This is your state of meditation.

Mindfulness and focus are the steps you climb to attain a state of meditation. Do not expect to hear voices, or instructions of where to go or what to do. As long as you become one with silence, you are at one with the universe. All that you desire; all that you work for; all that you need is transmitted in that moment of silence; and the answers you seek will be waiting for you at some point after your session. The answers, the things you ask for will begin to appear in the days that follow.

***

Make sure to check out the rest of the books in this series:

Fail Your Way to Success: The Definitive Guide to Failing Forward and Learning How to Extract the Greatness Within - Why Failing is an Integral Part of Success and Why You Should Never Fear it

https://www.amazon.com/dp/B0738WDK6W

Discipline Your Way to Success: The Definitive Guide to Success Through Self-Discipline - Why Self-Discipline is Crucial to Your Success Story and How to Take Control Over Your Thoughts and Actions

https://www.amazon.com/dp/B0741FMCBX

Ask Your Way to Success: The Definitive Guide to Success Through Asking - How to Transform Your Life by Learning the Art of Asking

https://www.amazon.com/dp/B074CJPFMH

Believe Your Way to Success: The Definitive Guide to Believing and Your Path to Success How Believing Takes You from Where You are to Where You Want to Be

https://www.amazon.com/dp/B0747N14KF

www.ingramcontent.com/pod-product-compliance
Lightning Source LLC
Chambersburg PA
CBHW021135300426
44113CB00006B/435